CLAIM YOUR FREE COLORING PAGES BELOW

ISBN: 978-1-7390959-5-6

CHIBI WICTHES

GLORIA JONES

TABLE OF

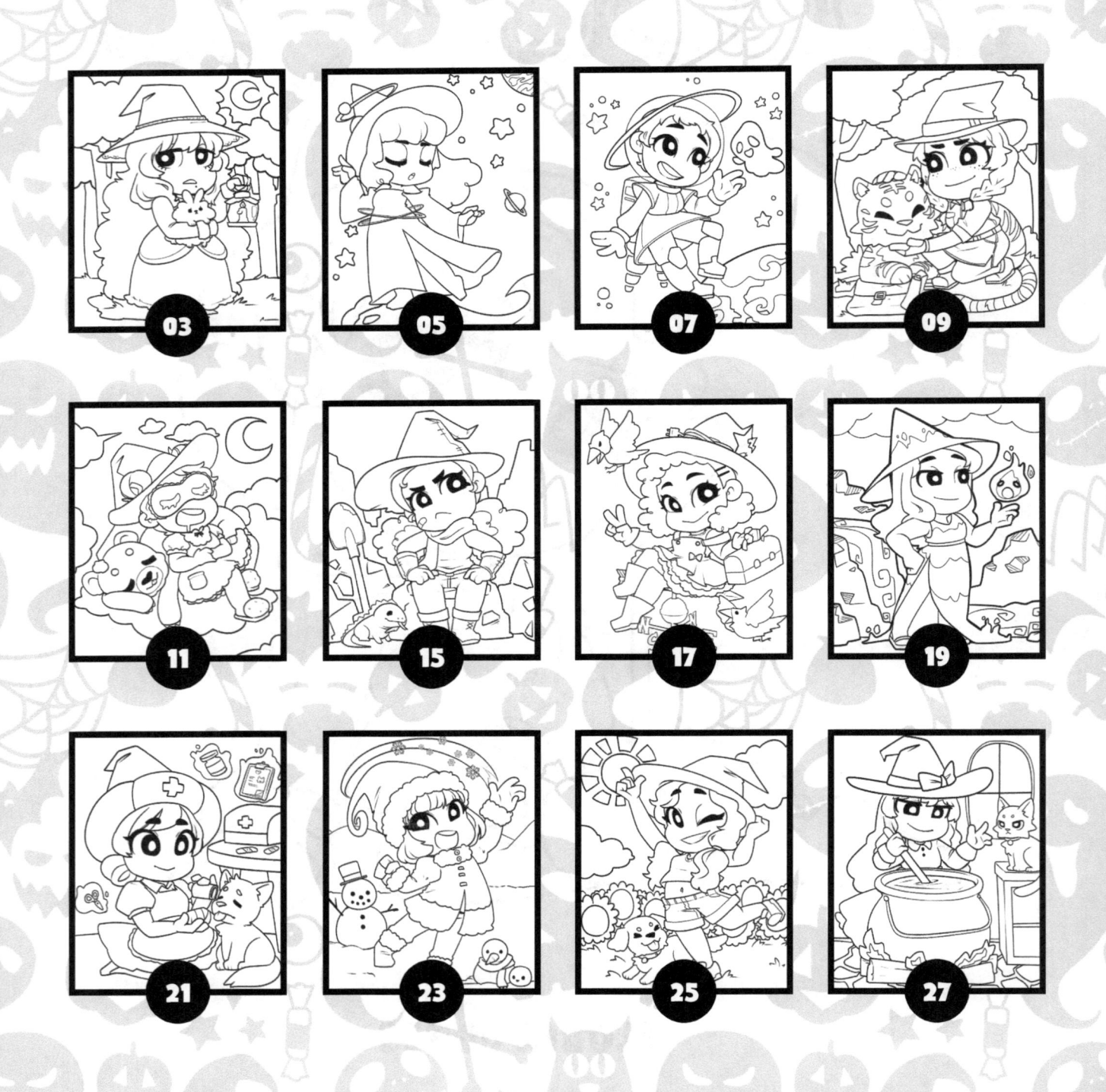

CONTENTS

BONUS PAGE!

CHAMELEON

PUBLICATIONS

COLORING

CAN ACTIVATE PARTS OF THE BRAIN LIKE A **CLICK** OF A **SWITCH!**

YOUR **CREATIVITY** GETS INSTANTLY **ACTIVATED** WHEN CHOOSING YOUR COLORS. YOUR **LOGIC** CAN ALSO BE ACTIVATED WHEN COLORING **SHAPES & FORMS**

SO IF HAVE A LOGICAL PROBLEM OR A CREATIVE PROBLEM ON YOUR MIND, COLORING COULD HELP SOLVE THAT FOR YOU.

32

CHAMELEON

PUBLICATIONS

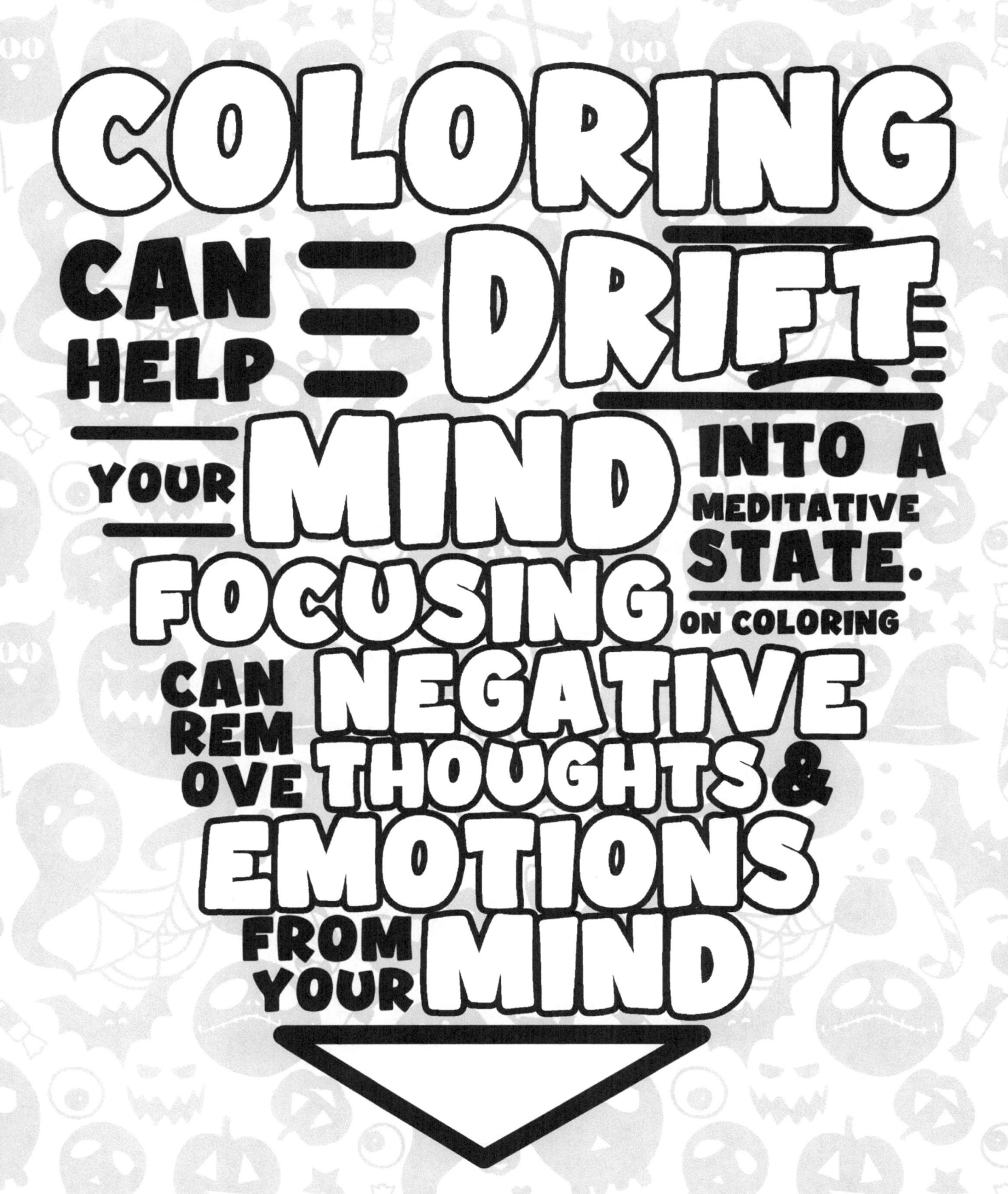

COLORING CAN HELP ≡ DRIFT YOUR MIND INTO A MEDITATIVE STATE. FOCUSING ON COLORING CAN REMOVE NEGATIVE THOUGHTS & EMOTIONS FROM YOUR MIND

SO LET'S COLOR!

38

★ BONUS PAGE ★

CHALLENGE

SO YOU THINK YOU CAN CREATE A BETTER COVER THAN US...

GO AHEAD, SHOW US WHAT YOU GOT!

CHAMELEON
PUBLICATIONS

SHOW THE WHOLE WORLD!
YOUR MASTERPIECE

LET THE WORLD DISCOVER YOUR ART BY UPLOADING YOUR CREATION WITH YOUR AMAZON REVIEW.

CHAMELEON
PUBLICATIONS

CLAIM YOUR FREE COLORING PAGES BELOW

DISCOVER YOUR NEXT ESCAPE

AVAILABLE ONLY AT

amazon

COLOR TEST

	#0000		

COLOR TEST

	#0000		

Made in United States
Troutdale, OR
10/01/2024

23307915R00038